Meditation For Beginners

Practical Meditation

How to Fight Stress, Anxiety and Depression to Live A Happy and Fulfilling Life with Meditation Even If You've Never Meditated Before

Antony Felix

Your Free Gift

As a way of thanking you for the purchase, I'd like to offer you a complimentary gift:

- **5 Pillar Life Transformation Checklist:** This short book is about life transformation, presented in bit size pieces for easy implementation. I believe that without such a checklist, you are likely to have a hard time implementing anything in this book and any other thing you set out to do religiously and sticking to it for the long haul. It doesn't matter whether your goals relate to weight loss, relationships, personal finance, investing, personal development, improving communication in your family, your overall health, finances, improving your sex life, resolving issues in your relationship, fighting PMS successfully, investing, running a successful business, traveling etc. With a checklist like this one, you can bet that anything you do will seem a lot easier to implement until the end. Therefore, even if you don't continue reading this book, at least read the one thing that will help you in every other aspect of your life. Grab your copy now by clicking/tapping here or simply enter http://bit.ly/2fantonfreebie into your browser. Your life will never be the same again (if you implement what's in this book), I promise.

PS: I'd like your feedback. If you are happy with this book, please leave a review on Amazon.

Introduction

Would you like to gain control over your automatic negative thoughts? Are you looking for an effective way to reduce stress and get into a state of profound, deep peace? Well, look no further, because meditation is what you need. Meditation is a simple and safe way to gain self-awareness.

This book aims to demystify the various myths surrounding meditation and equip you with practical tips on how to make meditation a part of your daily life.

In this book, you will discover the basics of meditation. You will also learn the benefits of meditation, how it improves your quality of life, and the various ways to practice meditation from the comfort of your home. Contrary to popular belief, you are about to discover that meditation is the simplest thing you could ever do to be present and happy without the need for external motivation or stimulation!

Table of Contents

Your Free Gift _____ 2

Introduction _____ 3

Chapter 1: What is Meditation? _____ 6

Chapter 2: History of Meditation _____ 8

Chapter 3: Science Proven Benefits of Meditation _____ 10

Chapter 4: How to Meditate Even If You've Never Meditated Before _____ 15

Chapter 5: Meditation Techniques _____ 19

   Mindfulness Meditation _____ 19

   Qigong _____ 26

   Walking Meditation _____ 28

   Mantra Meditation _____ 31

   Body Scan Meditation _____ 37

   Transcendental Meditation _____ 41

   Do Nothing Meditation _____ 44

   Meditate on Your Thoughts _____ 50

Chapter 6: Meditation Tips _____ 57

Chapter 7: Mudras to Strengthen the Effectiveness of Meditation _____ 66

Varada Mudra _____ 67

Samadhi Mudra _____ 68

Karana Mudra _____ 69

Jnana Mudra _____ 70

Varuna Mudra _____ 71

Gyan Mudra _____ 72

Prana Mudra _____ 73

Apana Mudra _____ 75

Shuni Mudra _____ 76

Conclusion _____ 78

Do You Like My Book & Approach To Publishing? _____ 79

1: First, I'd Love It If You Leave a Review of This Book on Amazon. _____ 79

2: Check Out My Emotional Mastery Books ____ 79

3: Grab Some Freebies On Your Way Out; Giving Is Receiving, Right? _____ 80

Chapter 1: What is Meditation?

Even though meditation seems to be growing in popularity, very few people have a true understanding of what meditation is or what it means to meditate. In fact, it is common to see meditation described as mental concentration on a certain object, or you can meditate by thinking about something that gives you satisfaction or peace.

While these techniques are ones you can use to slow down and bring the incessant activities in your mind to a complete halt, these exercises are not meditation per se; rather, they are what we can only describe as their substitutes since stopping our minds all-together is not possible.

Actually, meditation is not an act of doing. It is a state of thoughtless awareness irrespective of what you are doing. Thus, you are either in or not in this state. For instance, you can meditate while performing your daily chores, but at other times, you may find it difficult to meditate even when seated in the lotus posture in a tranquil environment! This means meditation is more than taking a moment to sit quietly or ponder.

Meditation is a state of profound, deep peace that arises whenever your mind is calm and silent, but fully alert. In simple terms, you can meditate by training your mind to focus on a particular object such as a thought, a word, or even an individual. Thus, you can use meditation to rest your mind and gain a state of awareness that differs from your usual waking state. In essence, meditation revolves around the beginning of an inner transformation that can propel you to a higher level of awareness where you can fulfill your true potential.

As you meditate, your mind must be clear, relaxed, and inwardly engrossed. You should be fully awake and alert but ensure that your mind does not pay attention to the external world; this helps you attain an inner calm and focused state that allows your mind a chance to become still. Thus, meditation only deepens when your mind becomes silent and no longer acts as a source of unnecessary distraction.

Having defined meditation, we now need to understand a bit of its background. You might be wondering how and why meditation has evolved to be so popular. To understand this, let us understand its history.

Chapter 2: History of Meditation

Even though the earliest historical records show that meditation was part of a Hindu tradition commonly called Vedantism, a tradition practiced around 1500 BCE, many historians believe meditation (as a practice) dates back to 3000 BCE.

Development of other forms of meditation occurred between 600 and 500 BCE as recorded in Buddhist India and Taoist China. Meditation must have been a significant component of the morality salvation formula, contemplative concentration, knowledge, and liberty.

The practice of meditation later spread via the Silk Road to other western cultures and influenced religions such as Judaism. In the 3rd Century AD, Plotinus developed meditation techniques.

While touring China in 653 AD, Dosho, A Japanese monk, discovered Zen. On his return to Japan, Dosho introduced meditation to the country by opening the first meditation hall.

From the 8th century AD, the practice of meditation grew significantly to a point where it formed an important part of the Japanese culture. However, as currently used, the terminology "to meditate," comes from the Latin word *meditatum,* which means, "to ponder", a concept introduced in 12th century AD.

Throughout the middle age, the practice of meditation grew and developed into different religious traditions. For instance, the Jews practiced meditation as a form of prayer.

Ancient meditation teachings began gaining popularity in the West in the 18th century. The 1927 publication of the "Tibetan Book of the Dead" attracted significant attention from the West thereby eliciting a lot of interest in the practice. The Insight Meditation Movement followed suit in the 1950s in Burma and advanced various studies on the benefits of meditation.

The 1958 publication of "The Dharma Bums" saw further attention on meditative practice. In 1978, researchers in the U.S. founded the Mindfulness-Based Stress Reduction (MBSR) program, a program that used meditation to treat patients suffering from various chronic diseases.

From then, meditation's popularity continues to thrive. A 2007 survey discovered that 1 in every 10 Americans has meditated at one point or the other. If you are wondering why meditation is becoming increasingly popular, let us look at some of the reasons why most people opt to practice meditation.

Chapter 3: Science Proven Benefits of Meditation

Meditation allows you to be still; it gives you a chance to examine what is within you. Learning to do this will help you gain the highest level of joy, a joy that is immense and persistent. By meditating, you can calm yourself, let go of biases, and objectively see things as they truly are.

Besides that, practicing meditation can be beneficial to you in the following ways:

1: Easing Chronic Back Pains

Lower back pains can be a nuisance that denies you the ability to be productive in your daily life. Back pains may occur because of stress, a lowered level of flexibility, poor muscle tone, poor posture, or a sedentary lifestyle. Normally, chronic back pains stem from muscle tension marked by prolonged muscle contraction that leads to severe pain.

If you seat for a very long time, your blood flow throughout the body reduces. If you spend a large portion of your week sitting, you will develop muscle weakness and imbalance meaning any over-compensation of activity during the weekend will lead to severe injuries. Using pain medications will only mask the problem instead of addressing the root cause.

The good news is that through meditation, you can achieve lasting and effective pain relief and remedy the underlying cause of the back pain. By meditating, you can relax the overly tense muscles and promote good blood circulation throughout the body. By meditating, you will also soothe the circuits that amplify the pains.

Meditation also helps you to increase awareness and acceptance of your feelings, whether physical discomfort or emotional pains. Hence, by meditating, you will be in a position to observe painful sensations as they rise and accept them for what they are no matter how painful they may be.

2: Stress Reduction

Studies show that practicing meditation for at least 10 minutes daily can help you achieve greater capacity for relaxation that is ideal for improved cardiovascular health, decreased anxiety, and improved stress control. Ordinarily, when your body encounters a sudden threat or stress, it activates a characteristic "fight or flight" response.

When active, this response causes the adrenal glands to releases epinephrine and norepinephrine hormones that lead to increased blood pressure, increased blood flow to muscles, faster breathing, and increased heartbeat. It is also important to note that you possess strong neural pathways that connect your bodily sensations and your brain's fear centers to the prefrontal cortex.

Meditation weakens these connections and helps you avoid reacting strongly to sensations that would have otherwise triggered your "fight or flight" response. Instead, the relaxation response occasioned by meditation elicits opposite bodily reactions, and your body enters into a state of deep relaxation marked by decreased metabolism, blood pressure, pulse, and breathing. This is because the connection between bodily sensations, fear centers, and the part of your brain responsible for reasoning strengthens, which engenders rational responses. Therefore, to enhance your mood, lower your blood pressure and reduce any lifestyle stress, train your body daily to get into this state of deep relaxation.

3: Slowed Aging

Studies show that meditating daily has the potential to revitalize the body more effectively than normal sleep. As noted above, meditation leads to reduced stress. Remember that stress has a significant effect on aging since it reduces your immunity as well as affects the digestive system. Meditation calms your body and mind and deters stress from wearing you down.

Meditation also boosts production of melatonin, a hormone manufactured in the brain by the pineal gland. Melatonin slows the aging process by activating and reenergizing your immune system, increasing production of cells in the bone marrow, regulating the circadian system, and acting as an effective antioxidant.

4: Improved Sleep

Sleep disturbances affect millions of people all over the world. The estimate is that half of those over the age of 55 experience sleep problems. When your mind preoccupies itself with all the problems you need to solve or things you need to do, sleep disturbances such as insomnia creep in.

In addition, excessive indulgence in unhealthy dietary habits, too much stimulation in the evenings through the computer or TV, inadequate rest, use of drugs, and overindulgence in stimulants such as coffee and tea, stress, and tension, stimulates your nervous system. However, you are likely to find meditation a reliable way to give your body or mind relief from stress and anxiety.

Meditation evokes the relaxation response, something often characterized by a deep physiological shift in your body. The primary aim of this physiological effect is to calm your brain's arousal system. By meditating regularly (say for at least 20 minutes daily), you can develop a balanced nervous system. Having adequate sleep enables your body to initiate its healing and restorative processes thereby reversing the physiological, biochemical and emotional effects of stress.

Other benefits of practicing meditation include enhanced mental focus, better performance at school or work, improvement of irritable bowel syndrome symptoms, enhanced personal confidence, and even reduced addiction cases.

NOTE: Even though meditation has many benefits, do not use meditation as a substitute for appropriate medical care. Still, take note that meditation may result in medical breakthroughs and even become therapeutic especially in cases where the use of conventional medical practices proves unsuccessful.

Surely, these benefits have given you the motivation you need to start practicing meditation. If you feel motivated and would like to get started, navigate to the next chapter where we shall discuss how to meditate:

Chapter 4: How to Meditate Even If You've Never Meditated Before

Over the years, meditation has evolved into various forms and types. However, the principle behind all forms of meditation remains the same. This chapter explores how to meditate and outlines how you can incorporate meditation into your daily schedule.

You may consider experimenting with the various types of meditation before settling on a technique that best suits you. If getting started on your own is a bit challenging, take advantage of the powerful experience of meditating in a group setting by attending a meditation class. In addition, consider having a teacher talk you through your preferred technique so that your experience can be easier and full of fun.

It is also important to note that to meditate, you do not necessarily need any equipment. That is the foolproof beauty and simplicity of meditation: Just prepare a quiet space and spare a few minutes each day and you are ready to meditate. To establish the habit, it is prudent to meditate at the same time every day. You can start committing as little as five minutes once or twice a day and gradually increase the time until you can comfortably meditate for an hour.

The secret to making meditation habitual is to increase the priority of meditation above all other activities in your life. You will only be successful if you put meditation ahead of work and other urgent commitments. Remember, consistency leads to perfection; let meditation form part of your daily habit. Skipping days all the time will not be helpful. You can only start getting the real benefits after weeks and months of consistency.

Inasmuch as meditation is extremely simple, it is also extremely difficult because at the initial stages, your mind is likely to be out of control and maintaining control over your mind for 5 seconds will be a monumental task. This can be very frustrating especially when you are eager to reap the benefits of meditation. Understand that this is normal. The reality is that this 'difficult nature' is humbling and will help you realize the amount of effort you need to develop self-control.

Below are general guidelines you can follow as you start meditating:

1: Look for a Meditation Place

You can designate a room, a space, or a corner within your room as your meditation spot/place. Use this space to build special feelings that help you enter into a meditative state as fast as possible. This spot should be distractions free.

While you are free to add objects that can help calm your mind and focus your practice, do not overdo it: keep the area simple and clutter free. Adding objects such as incense, flowers, religious symbols, a photo, and candles to your meditation spot is a good idea.

2: Sit Comfortably on the Floor or on a Chair

Your posture should be relaxed and upright. Just let your back remain as straight as possible as you sit perfectly still.

You can focus your gaze on an object of choice, or just close your eyes. This will help you concentrate and begin paying attention to your inner self.

3: Let Your Breathing Be Gentle, Deep and at a Slow Pace

Breathe consistently and use your diaphragm. You may also have to pay attention to your breathing; if you rarely breathe deeply, this is the time to start practicing.

4: Always Let Your Mind Remain Focused On the Object or Inward

Whenever your mind stops focusing on your point of focus, accept that it has done so and re-direct it back to your point of focus. To clear your mind, take note of all the thoughts that come up and then release them.

As you gain confidence in the practice, you will discover that you can meditate from anywhere: in the toilet, while on your bed, or even as you sit on your couch.

Let us now look at meditation techniques you can use to meditate.

Meditation For Beginners

Chapter 5: Meditation Techniques

The following are common forms of meditation:

Mindfulness Meditation

This type of meditation revolves around being mindful. You can use mindfulness meditation to heighten your awareness and acceptance of being in the present moment. The aim of this meditation technique is to broaden your conscious awareness by focusing on what you experience while meditating, like the way your breath flows.

To practice this meditation technique, just observe your thoughts and feelings and release them without passing judgment. You can perform mindfulness meditation as follows:

1: Sit On a Chair, a Cushion, or on the Floor

Your back should remain straight and unsupported. You may choose to sit in the lotus position (with legs crossed). You may even lie down, but take care that you do not fall asleep. Just find what feels natural to you and ensure you are as comfortable as possible. For instance, make sure the room temperature is adequate and your clothing comfortable.

2: Determine the Appropriate Length of Time

Start with five to ten minutes and gradually increase your time. Do not opt for long meditation session (especially as you get started): you do not want to feel overwhelmed. Just begin with shorter sessions and increase the time as needed. Setting a timer will keep you from constantly checking your time as you meditate. However, ensure the "end of meditation" timer is a gentle soothing sound like soft piano music instead of a jarring buzzer.

3: Relax and Settle Your Mind

If your day has been stressful, relaxing and settling will take a bit of time. At first, you will feel a little strange about meditation; this should not worry you. For instance, you may experience your emotions stirring and you can even begin to think about previous happenings or things that may happen in future. This is fine. Your mind is just dancing; let it dance for a few moments as you settle in. Use a few seconds to identify your feelings before shifting your focus to your physical position.

Take deep breaths and begin paying close attention to your breath, especially the way it moves. As you breathe in, are you aware that you are actually breathing in and when you breathe out, are you aware of what is actually happening?

Experience how every breath flows in and out of your body, how your lungs fill up with air and the subsequent release of air through your throat and mouth. To relax and settle better, you can lengthen and deepen each breath. At this point, take note that by observing your breath, you are practicing mindfulness.

As you meditate, if you notice unpleasant emotions or thoughts, do not focus on them: release them. Whenever you come across your mental stream of thoughts and emotion, avoid beating yourself up. Just train yourself to let go of such emotions without judgment.

4: Whenever You Encounter Distractions, Always Return To Your Breath

Your mind will oscillate between the future and the past. You may experience unpleasant thoughts or emotions, or disturbing noises may interrupt you. When this happens, simply go back to observing your inhalations and exhalations.

As you focus on your breathing, always aim for neutrality. If thoughts arise, maintain the culture of not passing judgment. Do not even start judging how you are meditating. Just know that meditation and distractions are two pieces of one. Remember that one of your primary goals is to remain focused on the present moment.

As you start mastering this technique, you can make it part of your daily life. For instance:

Try Eating Mindfully

Mindful eating helps you slow down, chew gradually, and enjoy the food. Take an apple and practice mindful eating as follows:

1. Pick up the apple, stare at it, and find out its texture and form. Start feeling the apple in your hands.

2. Move it closer to your face and try to smell it for a moment. Take note of how your body responds, i.e. are you craving a bite? Are you salivating?

3. Bite the apple and take note of its taste. How does it feel? Are you enjoying as you chew it?

4. As you take one bite after another, chew it as well as you can, at least 25 times and focus on the texture of the bite that you feel in your mouth, the taste of every bite and the aroma you can smell. Engage yourself in the experience by perceiving every bite as an experience on its own. This makes you appreciate each bite that you take and be grateful for it. Plus, it promotes satiety.

5. If you do not like the taste of the food, do not refer to it as bad. Instead, try to come up with more suitable adjectives according to the experience you have. For instance, if the spaghetti you are having is bland, call it bland and tasteless. If you just took a bite of an apple and it somehow tastes bitter, call it bitter. This simple practice makes you perceive an experience for what it is and keeps you from associating unnecessary meaning and labels with things. It also helps you build a nonjudgmental and more accepting attitude.

6. When you finish your meal, end it on a note of gratitude and feel thankful for the meal you had. However it was, it filled up your tummy and helped you survive so you must acknowledge it.

7. Make sure to work on these guidelines every time you sit down for a meal.

You will have to consciously remind yourself to eat mindfully for a couple of weeks to nurture the habit of mindful eating. Also, try to eat without any sort of screen in front of you because when you are watching a video or a show on TV or your tablet, you become distracted and focus more on watching than eating. This makes you simply gulp down one bite after another in a rather mechanical manner instead of actually eating, enjoying the meal and appreciating it.

Unconscious eating is one of the biggest contributors to weight management issues. Often, many of us complain of our struggle with weight loss. While we whine, we fail to take notice of our eating habits that are mostly unhealthy and focus primarily on filling our tummies with food and not actually eating and enjoying it.

Make sure to always add a small portion of food to your plate and eat it mindfully, taking one small bite after another, chewing it properly and then taking another bite. Think about whether you need another bite or not and then take one. The same applies to having another serving. Ask yourself if you really need a second helping of a meal and if your tummy does rumble for real, take another small serving. When you tune into your feelings and body every time before eating, you are likely to eat only when you really need to and not at all times. This promotes contentment and satiety that helps you manage your weight easily and get rid of all the stress associated with that problem.

Walk Mindfully

Meditate as you walk. Start walking and as you do, pay attention to how it feels. Feel how your muscles stretch, bend, and move. Try to walk barefoot and do so slowly so that you can focus on your movements and the sensation of your feet touching and leaving the ground. Notice the texture and temperature of the ground as well.

Focusing On Feelings and Sensations

When you are feeling pain, you can practice mindfulness as a way to reduce tension and pain in your body. Decide on the body part you want to focus on. It could be an external or internal part. Note the kind of sensations arising from it, whether pleasant, neutral, or unpleasant. Take note of how your mind and body interact with these sensations. Continue doing this on all body parts as if you are conducting a body scan. Keep observing the various sensations and allowing them to pass.

Consider Brushing Your Teeth Mindfully

Taste the toothpaste; feel your toothbrush's bristles and your hand's motion. You can also drive, talk and even shower mindfully. When talking, try to focus on the words you are uttering, how you speak those words, and ensure your listening is full of presence and attention. Just remember that all you need to do is be present. Do not deliberately add anything to your present moment experiences; instead, become fully aware of what is going on without losing yourself in anything that may arise from time to time.

Qigong

Qigong is of Chinese origin and is a body-mind exercise meant for martial arts training, meditation, and overall good health. Key Qigong characteristics include regulated breathing, inner focus, and slow body movement.

You can practice qigong through a dynamic set of movements or in a static position such as standing or sitting. However, sitting is the only posture recommended if you are practicing qigong for meditation. You can practice seated qigong meditation as follows:

1. Sit comfortably. Center and balance your body.

2. Get into a relaxed state. Let all your internal organs, nerves, and muscles be in a state of full relaxation.

3. Start regulating your breathing. Your breathing should be deep, long, and soft.

4. Compose yourself and let your mind be as calm as possible.

5. Focus your attention on the "lower dantian." Lower dantian refers to your body's center of gravity; it is 2 inches below the navel. By so doing, you are accumulating and rooting the vital energy known as the qi. The idea is that where you focus your mind and attention is where your qi is. Therefore, by paying attention on the dantian, you are simply accumulating your vital energy in such a natural reservoir.

6. Finally, feel the vital energy (qi) as it flows freely all over your body.

Walking Meditation

Practice walking meditation as a complement to your seated meditation. Walking meditation is more than strolling in the park. It involves slow walks carried out in coordination with breathing or particular focusing exercises. It differs from seated meditation in that while walking, your eyes remain open as your body moves. You can interact with the external world and you can be mindful of your body sensations and remain anchored to the present moment. Below are guidelines for walking meditation:

1. Choose a suitable place. The place should be safe and free from distractions or disturbances. Avoid high traffic or heavily populated walking areas. Your backyard is a good place to start.

2. Walking meditations can last 15 minutes. However, you can do it for longer periods since there are no discomforts of immobility.

3. Ensure your pace is slow, steady, and even. If your ability to focus is weak or your mind feels agitated, walking very slowly will help you stay in the present moment and focus easily with each step.

4. Before starting off, take a few minutes to breathe deeply and anchor your attention in your body. Anchor yourself as follows:

   - Get into a hip-width stance; your weight must balance evenly on your feet.

- Breathe deeply for several moments.
- Close your eyes and then scan your entire body starting from your feet. Take note of any feelings, thoughts, and sensations and spend some time exploring them fully.
- Direct your awareness to your body and get to know how your body feels while standing; try to become aware of all your body sensations.

5. Keep refocusing your attention. Focus your attention on your walking and breathing.

There are very many forms of walking meditation such as Theravada, Zen, Mindfulness, Daoist, and Yoga. Follow the steps below to practice Zen walking meditation:

1. Stand straight; your back should be upright but not rigid.
2. Make sure you are feeling your feet as they touch the ground. Your weight must remain evenly distributed.
3. Bend in the left thumb and wrap your fingers over it before placing it slightly above your belly button. Get your right hand wrapped around it, with the right thumb resting in the gap formed between your index finger and the left thumb in what we call *shashu*.

Meditation For Beginners

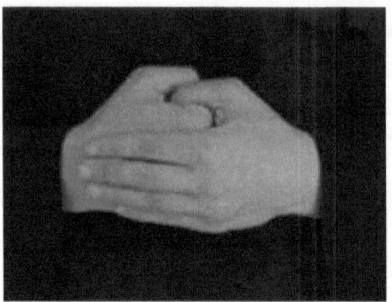

4. Let your eyes stare about 5 or 6 feet in front but do not focus on anything.

5. After each complete breath, take a small step. Begin with the right leg: your steps should be the length of your foot.

6. Let your body and mind walk and breathe in a well-balanced way and your focus be on your breathing and steps. The idea is to walk clockwise, especially around the room.

Mantra Meditation

A mantra is a suggestion that you chant over and over again to imbed it in your subconscious mind. Your subconscious creates your internal program based on the suggestions you provide it with. If you focus on self-defeating statements and keep thinking about how stressed you feel all the time, you will only encourage your subconscious to focus on that. Your subconscious mind then creates more thoughts based on those ideas which then travel out in the universe and draw similar thoughts and experiences towards them. So if you fixate on stress, anxiety and how incapable you are in life; that is what you will get in return.

To overcome your stress, anxiety, depression and everything else that is obstructing your way towards happiness, train your subconscious to think positively and in terms of that particular goal. For that, you need to modify the way you talk to yourself as your self-talk is a huge contributor to low self-esteem and in turn stress. If you keep saying self-depreciating and demeaning things to yourself, you will only think negatively about yourself that in turn will make your subconscious focus on negativity.

An effective way to build positive self-talk is to practice mantra meditation. It requires you to chant a positive mantra time and again, and completely focus on it to affirm it to your subconscious mind. Affirming something means you put your complete faith in the suggestion and believe it to be the ultimate truth. The constant repetition of a particular suggestion compels your subconscious to embrace the suggestion so it then imbeds it in your internal program. Once a suggestion becomes a part of your program, it then turns into your belief and helps you think in that direction. This means that if you constantly tell yourself that you feel peaceful, you will believe that and will attract different thoughts and positive experiences your way that will help you attain the peace you desire. The same applies for happiness, confidence, wealth, abundance, love and any other goal you wish to actualize.

Here is how you can practice mantra meditation.

- Think of the improvement you would like to bring in yourself or any goal you wish to achieve. If you wish for happiness, that could be your goal; if you want to overcome stress, you could create a mantra around it.

- Create a short, positive mantra based on your goal. It could be a word or a phrase suggesting the goal you'd like to fulfill. For instance, to find inner peace, you could chant 'peace', or to let go of anxiety, you could say, 'I feel at peace in every moment that I experience.'

- Ensure your mantra is a positive one, succinct and delivers the right message to your mind. If you wish to be happy, say 'I am happy' instead of 'I do not wish to be sad.' Our subconscious does not really comprehend words with a negative connotation and omits them from a suggestion so the 'not' in the suggestion above is likely to be omitted and the suggestion will be changed to 'I wish to be sad.' To better understand this, think of how you always do things you are told not to engage in. That's because your mind does not accept that 'no' and makes you do exactly what you are forbidden to do. To ensure you don't keep feeling sad and stressed, come up with a purely positive suggestion that only suggests you are happy.

- Additionally, your suggestion needs to be present oriented, which means it must suggest that you have achieved your goal in the present. If you want to overcome depression, say 'I feel healthy and happy' instead of saying 'I want to be healthy.' Your subconscious cannot distinguish between reality and imagination, and accepts whatever you frequently suggest it. If you suggest that you wish to be happy, it will focus on bringing you happiness in the future and you will be deprived of it in your present. That said, if you suggest that you are happy now, it will believe that and focus on bringing you the happiness you aspire for.

- Once your affirmation is ready, you need to sit back comfortably and relax in your meditation spot and calm down. You can begin with mindfulness meditation and after a minute or two of practicing it, bring every ounce of your attention to your breath.

- Observe your breath for a few moments as peacefully and nonjudgmentally as possible, and then slowly start chanting your chosen mantra. You can say it out loud or in your head, but for starters, it is best to chant it openly and loudly so you focus on it better. If it is a word, focus on every syllable peacefully and completely and allow its vibration to fully ring in your ears. If it is a phrase, utter every word slowly, clearly and confidently so you focus on it completely and make it imbed in your head.

- Keep chanting the mantra over and over again, taking your time with every word and only focusing on it as you say it.

- You may wander off in thought, but that is okay. Every time, you feel distracted, gently bring back your attention to your breath and the mantra you are chanting and focus on it. Do that a couple of times and you'll find yourself becoming more attentive to the practice.

- When you end the practice, softly stop uttering the mantra and relax. Gradually, bring back your attention to the present and give yourself time to settle into the real world.

Practice this exercise for 5 to 15 minutes daily to energize yourself and focus your subconscious mind on the positive things around you.

You can build mantras on confidence, peacefulness, success, abundance, love and anything you wish to accomplish and chant them repeatedly to accomplish your desired goal.

Make sure you inject your belief in the practice when you do it by visualizing what you chant. If you are chanting a mantra based on happiness, imagine yourself being the happiest version of yourself. Add details in the imagination such as sights, sounds, feelings, emotions, expressions and textures to engage your sense in the experiences and become fully immersed in it. The more you believe it, the more engrossed you will become in it, the quicker you will engrain that suggestion in your subconscious to draw great experiences your way.

Take Action

it is important to highlight here the importance of taking meaningful action along with thinking positively and chanting happy mantras. Taking action is crucial to rewiring your mind to think optimistically and realistically, and not fall into the trap of negative, unconstructive thinking. That said, walking the walk is even more crucial in order to drive the desired results.

Once you encourage yourself to think positively, you must take the necessary action to support your positive frame of mind. If you constantly chant 'I am happy' then you need to do things that make you happy as well. If painting brings you pure joy, paint more and allow yourself to feel and enjoy everything that you paint. Allow yourself to paint anything that comes to you and let your emotions out through different colors. If dancing relaxes you, dance whenever you feel like and give your pain a positive outlet to eject from your body.

Meditation For Beginners

Make a list of whatever brings you happiness and engage in those practices on a regular basis. Similarly, analyze all those things that you are already engaged in that do nothing but strain your mind. For instance, you may have a habit of overthinking and that may be contributing to your chronic stress; or you may be hanging out a lot with negative influences and that maybe increasing the burden on your mind.

Closely observe yourself and your behavior, and slowly cut back on all the practices and engagements that hold you back. Be mindful of your behavior just as you are mindful of your thoughts and slowly change them for the better to unlock the happiness you truly deserve.

The same rules apply for achieving wealth, peace, abundance, success etc.- find out your mistakes and improve on them and engage in practices that would actually yield the outcomes you are looking for. Do that mindfully on a regular basis and you will achieve your goals for sure.

Body Scan Meditation

A great deal of stress and anxiety in our life comes from feeling unhappy with ourselves particularly our appearance. Even if we deny it, the truth is we do worry about how we look and oftentimes, it is the society that forces us to focus too much on our outward outlook instead of our inward appearance.

Body-shaming has sadly become quite a common phenomenon, one that has affected almost all of us at some point in our lives. We have been criticized for how we look, for the color of our skin, for being too chubby or too thin, for not being how we are expected to look like and for things we have no control over.

This only negatively influences our self-esteem making us devalue ourselves. Naturally, when we don't nurture self-respect, we feel stressed from within which then manifests itself in different ways. The frustration that we often experience and the anger that we vent on others is often courtesy of our low self-esteem.

To be happy and stress-free, we need to feel accepted and loved, and not just by those around us, but first by ourselves. You need to accept yourself the way you are and shower affection on yourself first if you wish to achieve improvement in any way. If you criticize yourself, you will only fall deeper into the dark abyss of negativity.

While chanting positive mantras based on acceptance and self-love are a great way to embrace yourself, you should also practice body scan meditation which is one of the most relaxing meditation techniques and does wonders in helping you build a great warm bond with yourself particularly your body.

What it Does?

Body scan meditation requires you to tune into your body, get comfortable with it and figure out the areas that are most affected by stress, negativity and anything else that causes you discomfort. It allows you to slowly relieve stress from those areas and build a better understanding of them.

For instance, if you suffer from chronic neck and shoulder pain, you can relax these areas by focusing on them and understanding the root cause of your stress. You then slowly mitigate the stress by relaxing your body and breathing it all out.

Also as you focus on building a healthier relationship with your body by accepting different parts as they are, you let go of ill feelings and achieve peace of mind.

Now that you know what body scan does for you, let us learn how to practice it.

How to Practice it

- Spread your exercise mat on the floor in your meditation spot and lie down on it comfortably. If lying on the floor feels uncomfortable because of any back problem or any other issue, lie down on your bed.

- Relax by practicing mindfulness meditation and taking deep breaths for a few minutes. Allow yourself to become grounded to the present moment and center yourself. This takes a couple of minutes so be patient with yourself.

- When you feel better, slowly bring your attention to your toes if you would like to work your way up from your toes to your head. If, however, you would like to focus on any one area in particular that is engulfed in pain or stress, or any area that you have trouble accepting and one that you have been body shamed for, pick that first.

- If you are observing your body to relieve stress, focus on any sensation, feeling or emotion you can sense in that area and think of how it makes you feel. If there is a tingling sensation in your toes, observe it mindfully and think of what caused it. As you scan it, keep breathing deeply and imagine the sensation slowly fading away with every deep exhale that you take. Do this for a few minutes or until the time you actually feel that area becoming relaxed and then move to the next part.

- If you are scanning a body part to improve your relationship with it, think of how you feel about it and what makes you nurture an ill feeling towards it. If you have been often criticized or bullied for your flabby arms and you hate them for that reason, focus on them. Think of how your arms add value to your life and if they are flabby, that's maybe because you did not take better care of your health. Also, think of how your body is yours to love and take care of and not to criticize and hate.

- Tell yourself that you love and accept your body no matter what and slowly chant or think 'I love and accept my body and my (body part you don't like)' over and over again.

- Make a mental image of embracing that body part and living a healthier life to take better care of it.

- You then need to work in the same way on another body part and so on until you get rid of ill feelings associated with your entire body. You can target one part in one session or work on the entire body in a 30 to 60 minute long sensation- do whatever works for you and feels easy.

Ensure you make this a regular practice and not a one-off thing because it is only by scanning your body regularly that you will be able to release all sorts of ill feelings and stress from it and build a better bond with it.

Transcendental Meditation

Abbreviated as TM, transcendental meditation uses a mantra and has sessions lasting 15-20 minutes. If you opt for this type of meditation, you must practice it twice daily on an empty stomach, preferably before dinner and breakfast. Traditionally, you can only learn TM by attending a course instructed by a qualified teacher. With that said, the following steps introduce you to TM:

1. Sit comfortably; you can sit in the lotus pose or any other comfortable pose.

2. Take 3 deep breaths and close your eyes. Continue breathing slowly so that you can relax fully.

3. With your eyes closed, start repeating a mantra in your mind. Do not verbalize the mantra; try rolling up your tongue whenever you find yourself verbalizing it.

4. As you speak the mantra in your mind, feel it. Do not concentrate on the word itself.

5. Silently chant the mantra for about 20 minutes. Try to feel your closeness and oneness with nature or the universe. As you meditate, your mind will interchangeably go through 4 mental states in no particular order. These states are:

   - Mantra only
   - Thought only

- Coexistence of mantra and thought
- No thought or mantra

As a beginner, you will not experience the fourth state especially in your first attempts. If you do not experience it, do not beat yourself up; this is normal and you must realize that this state is not one you can realize through conscious effort. Only regular meditation can help you get there and once you experience it, rejoice.

As you meditate, avoid holding onto the mantra. The idea is to repeat it silently without paying attention to it. Holding onto the word will keep you from experiencing the other states throughout your meditation session. You can tell if you are holding onto a mantra when you notice your mind repeating the mantra for too long.

Do not worry if your mind wanders or preoccupies itself with thoughts especially if you are not aware that you are thinking. When this happens, start again and concentrate on your mantra.

Always let the mantra fade away to experience the first 3 states interchangeably. Remember that every mental state forms part of the TM technique and as such, no state is right or wrong. Just let the mental states interchange so that you can experience the fourth state characterized by neither thoughts nor mantra.

If done properly, TM allows your body to settle down and get into a state of profound rest and relaxation since your mind experiences a state of complete inner peace without any effort or concentration on your part.

Do Nothing Meditation

Spiritual sages and meditation practitioners strongly believe that the highest state of deep spiritual awakening is switched on in complete awareness at all times. This suggests that the pure state of enlightenment has been there always, is still present and will forever be there. This is referred to as the 'Buddha Nature' in Buddhism and the 'true self' in Hinduism and other cultures. This means that through meditation our focus needs to be to cultivate a state of pure awakening that does not fade away once the meditative practice is over. That true sense of awakening must persist at all times. According to meditation experts, the 'Do Nothing' meditation is one such meditative technique that aims to do that.

The 'Do Nothing' meditation is known as 'shikantaza' in Zen Buddhism and as 'dzogchen' in Tibetan Buddhism. The renowned meditation teacher Krishnamurti referred to it as 'choice-less awareness.' Whatever the name you choose to call it by, its meaning remains the same- awaken your true spiritual self by doing nothing and just hanging in the present moment with an unbiased, peaceful sense of awareness.

The practice is rooted in the belief that while complete awakening is present in our minds at every single moment, many of us often struggle with truly experiencing it and being connected to it.

One major obstruction that gets in our way is to be an actual doer. Since we are always actively engaged in something and are always doing something, we believe that is the way to go about things. 'Doer-ship' (the state of constantly doing something) is at the core of our sense of self and is the heart of our ego. It is only by letting go of that sense of constantly putting in some effort, always trying to do something and pushing yourself forward that you allow yourself to relax, diminish your ego and just be present in the moment. To simplify it, the sense of complete volition is what the sense of self is about and when you let go of it, you allow yourself to live in the moment without any judgment and bias.

The Neuroscience behind the Practice

The 'do nothing' meditation is backed by science and there is substantial neuroscience behind it. There is a structure in our brain known as the posterior cingulate cortex (PCC) that has a big role to play in our default mode network (DMN) which is triggered on whenever we engage in thoughts related to ourselves or whenever we get distracted from a task.

A study shows that the DMN activity is correlated with a negative effect that means that this preoccupation with our thoughts makes us feel bad. Brain scans prove that the PCC activity decreases when you shun the feeling of doing anything at all. When you feel things around you are happening effortlessly, your default mode network and PCC, both relax making you feel good about yourself. This feeling of allowing things to flow effortlessly is a hallmark of the peak experience or the flow state. Mostly peak experiences take place when we have practiced something for years. However, when you just allow yourself to be in the moment and let things unfold naturally, you reach the flow state easily, quickly and effortlessly. During this process, it is highly likely for you to tap into your truly awakened mind and recognize it.

How to Practice it

Practicing the 'do nothing' technique is easy and difficult at the same time. Easy because it actually *requires you to do nothing at all*, but difficult because doing nothing does not come easy to many of us. Even when we are doing nothing, we are doing something. We are worrying about something, we are thinking about something, we are making plans, we are recalling memories and we are fretting about why we are not doing something.

Although the meditative techniques taught previously allow you to relax and unlock that sense of mindfulness you need to live a truly awakened life, they give you some small tasks to do such as focusing on your breathing, chanting a mantra, observing something and so on. This feeds into the default mindset you have; you need to do something to be mindful and to meditate.

While all the meditative techniques taught so far are incredible and extremely effective, the do nothing practice goes a step further and pushes you to unleash your sense of awareness by simply doing nothing. This is why it feels hard and strange at first because you have to fight your urge of constantly doing and thinking something to just be in the moment. You need to just sit down, fight all those urges and do nothing. Here is how to go about this meditation technique:

- Sit in your meditation spot and relax yourself. If it helps, you can begin with mindfulness meditation to ground yourself to the present moment.

- You then need to slowly let go of any urge, any thought, any distraction and anything else that disturbs you and simply be in the moment.

- Whenever the thought of you getting caught up in something pops up, just let go of that.

- If you notice that you are trying to do something, let go of that feeling too.

- If an emotion bubbles up and you start to focus on that, slowly allow it to move outside of your system.

- If you feel you are struggling to be in the moment, remind yourself of how you just need to sit and not struggle with anything. It is actually that simple. When you stop fighting the urge to focus on the practice and not worry about anything, and allow every thought, every emotion, every disturbance, every feeling to exit your system with every breath you take, you slowly train yourself to do nothing and be present in the moment.

- Do not pay any attention to any sort of sensation, muscle tightening, constriction or any movement in your body.

Meditation For Beginners

Just be in the moment for about 2 to 5 minutes and when the timer beeps, open your eyes if you had closed them.

When the practice ends, you will notice that while you did not do anything special per say, you feel a lot calmer and focused than before and that is because you did nothing, but just appreciated the moment and tried to be aware of it.

The true sense of mindfulness is unlocked when you allow yourself to connect to the moment and not any thought, emotion, feeling or sensation and if you regularly practice the do nothing technique, you will definitely unleash that state of mind.

Practice it for 2 to 5 minutes at least thrice every week along with all the other meditative techniques that you do. You can start your meditation journey with it, or you can bring it in your routine after you have adjusted to the idea of meditation by practicing the other techniques for a couple of weeks. For the majority of people, it is hard to simply do nothing at all and if you fall in that category, it is best you begin with the other practices and once you build a somewhat habit of meditation for 5 minutes daily, you can move on to the 'do nothing' practice. Remember, even after practicing the other exercises, the do nothing technique may seem tough in the beginning, but it is only by doing it regularly and with determination that you will unlock within you the state of complete awakening, relaxation and the ability to open to the natural flow of things.

Once you start to better unlock this state of purity and enlightenment, and as you strengthen your state of mindfulness by working on all the techniques taught so far, you should start meditating on your thoughts. Clarity in life comes only with reflecting on yourself, your thoughts, your feelings and your aspirations. We complain of how our lives lack meaning, but still we do not pause to reflect on our wants, needs, wishes and ambitions. We just keep doing what we have built the habit of doing and do not stop to think of what we truly wish to do. This is why we feel incomplete, unsettled and chaotic. This feeling can only be eradicated and improved on if you meditate on your thoughts. The next chapter explores this very practice and helps you unlock that very clarity and sense of direction that is missing from your life.

Meditate on Your Thoughts

Buddha once wisely said,

"What you think, you become. What you feel, you attract. What you imagine, you create."

Your life is a manifestation of your thoughts. If you are not too pleased with the current state of your life and wish for things you haven't yet achieved, it is time to reflect on your thoughts.

We lack the meaning, value and empowerment we need in our lives to feel content, fulfilled, happy and peaceful. That said, we do not reflect on ourselves, our thoughts, our behavior and our decisions to find out what really went wrong. We say we aren't too happy with our career, relationships, decisions and choices in life, but do we ever sit back to think on what we truly want? Sadly, the answer is a big NO!

You need clarity, focus and direction in life from A to Z. You need to know exactly what you want, why you want it and how to achieve it to carve your path from zero to infinity. Only if you have clarity about your aspirations, your goals and your purpose in life, even the sky won't be the limit for you. You would know what you want and how to get there. Even if you falter along the way, you won't stop because you would believe in your goal and would keep finding newer, alternative routes to get to your destination.

But how can you attain that clarity? How can you figure out the missing link from your life? How can you find out what precisely you must do to shape your life into exactly how you envisage it? This is where meditation comes in handy. Just like meditation can help you become peaceful, happy, mindful and content, it can assist you in finding your sole purpose in life.

Sally, 28 is a fitness and wellness coach and is extremely proud of herself and pleased with her career choice. She has several high profile clients who are nothing but pleased with her work and choose to come back to her only over the years. While Sally is thriving in her professional life as well as her personal life, things weren't as great for her 5 years back. Half a decade ago, she was stuck in a terrible sales job that she hated and a relationship that was purely toxic and controlling. She didn't know what to do. There came once a point when she felt an inclination to engage in self-harming behaviors, but luckily for her, better sense prevailed and with the help of her supportive brother, she was introduced to meditation.

Slowly, Sally began to meditate and after a month of exercising simple breathing and mantra meditation techniques, she became calm enough to meditate on her thoughts. It was only when she meditated on her thoughts that she realized her entire life was in conflict with her core values and beliefs. With time and practice, she became more mindful of herself, her genuine desires and her truest aspirations. That knowledge helped her identify her life's vision and mission, and she then devised a plan of action to achieve that. This decision required her to completely transform her life and make strong, bold decisions. She had to do things she had never dreamt of, face and overcome her fears that were crippling her from within, but she did it because she was clear on what she wanted.

It took her a good 18 months to change her life the way she planned to and at the end, she was nothing, but proud of her decisions. She realized she wanted to pursue a career in health, fitness and wellness and had to get out of the toxic relationship to reclaim her life and so she did. When she looks back at her life, she only feels delighted and content.

Sally's life is just one of the millions who have benefitted from meditation. If they can achieve the tranquility and success they yearned for through the power of meditation so can you. Now that you know the wonders meditation can do for you, let us guide you on how to attain them.

How to Meditate on Your Thoughts

- Sit in your meditation spot and relax. Now that you know how to practice the 'do nothing' technique, exercise that to become grounded and at peace.

- Think of any problematic area in your life, one that is your top-most concern at the moment and one that you are eager to transform as soon as possible. It could be your health if you are suffering from an ailment or are at high risk of acquiring a health condition. It could be wealth and abundance if you are cash-strapped and tired of living from paycheck to paycheck. It could be spirituality if you feel throttled from within and want to be connected to your inner self. It could be your love life if you yearn for a loving partner you feel emotionally, physically and mentally bonded to. It could be your relationships if you are missing out on healthy, warm, nourishing and supportive loved ones. It could be precisely anything that makes you feel incomplete, disturbed and frustrated.

- It is best to have your journal and a pen at this point because reflecting on your thoughts becomes even easier and helpful when you write them down and record them. Writing down things solidifies them and gives you something to go through time and again to get more clarity.

- Once you have selected an area that you would like to explore, you need to get more specific about it. Every area mentioned above is an entire subject on its own and each one of us is likely to have dissimilar problems in it. You need to figure out exactly what upsets you in that area to become aware of your deepest pain point. For instance, if you are financially unstable, figure out the kind of stability you wish to have. Do you wish to have just enough money to pay your debts or do you want to amass wealth so that you never have to worry about any purchase ever? If you aren't too satisfied with your profession, do you just wish to change your industry, or do you wish to quit your job for good and become an entrepreneur? Keep asking yourself questions related to what pains you and why it pains you to get a better idea of what you genuinely want. A vague goal won't get you anywhere so this is the right time to cultivate the awareness and lucidity to move forward easily.

- Ask yourself questions such as: Why am I not happy with this thing? What do I want from it? What is it that my heart yearns? What will add value to my life? What is my heart longing for? What can I do to make things right?

- Take your time with each question and dig as deeper into it as possible. It is perfectly fine if you explore only one question in a 10 to 30 minute long session because the deeper you dig into a question, the more clearness you will attain. Don't forget to jot everything down.

- It is also important to keep your talents, skills and any capabilities that you have into account while deciding a career pathway if that is what you are exploring. You need know to what you are good at to better figure out an income channel that can give you a good return. Reflect on any of your passions and accomplishments at this time too. You need to know what adds excitement and value to your life, and what you can excel at to identify a clearer direction in life, and this is not just limited to your professional choices.

- Write down all your findings and reflect on it with deep clarity and unbiased attitude. Remember to explore different ideas when analyzing a question. If you are thinking of what career pathway to choose and an idea related to a field you have never ventured into pops up, do not disregard it. Meditation teaches you acceptance, peace and objectivity and if you do not apply that to your findings, you will never be able to put them to good use. If you have earlier believed a certain idea or an option to be redundant, nurture a more accepting attitude towards it now. If you had always believed that getting a degree was the only surefire way to get a good job, try thinking about it differently now. Do not shatter your whole belief system instantly because it will be tough and overwhelming, but do consider the possibility of trying new things. There is no harm in exploring different options and being open to new ideas because it is only through experimentation that you find what you truly want and are good at. You may have discarded a certain idea that did not appeal to you before, but if it seems plausible now, explore it.

Once you carry out a session of deep, reflective thinking on your thoughts, you need to go through the account time and again to establish nexus between different factors and connect the puzzle pieces together. This is how you will get the clarity that is currently missing out from your life. Remember to make this a consistent practice and not a one-off thing. You must meditate on your thoughts at least once a week for 30 to 60 minutes instead of doing it once in a blue moon because it is only through regular introspection that you will be able to make startling discoveries about your life that will actually make a positive difference in it.

Meditation is a healthy activity you can use to train your mind and gain full control of your life. There are many ways to practice meditation as you have learned. Do not be shy from exploring as many techniques as possible. Your main goal should be to find the one technique that fits your needs.

Chapter 6: Meditation Tips

As you read this book, you may have been wondering how you can make meditation part of your lifestyle without falling prey to random disruptions that inescapably creep up as you embark on this practice.

The following tips will help you overcome problems that may make meditation seem a daunting and less attractive activity:

1: Begin by Setting a Low Threshold Meditation Goal

Even though longer meditation sessions yield deeper peace, expecting a beginner to meditate for an hour is a tall order. Starting small proves more manageable and effective. You can start meditating for 3-5 minutes or even less. Surprisingly, 3 minutes of meditation may even appear to be a long time for a beginner. Remember, meditation is not a performance: you do not have to cover a given time duration for the sake of it.

Working with minor time increments will keep you motivated. In addition, keep focusing on the eventual benefits of meditation so that you can remain focused and be motivated to invest more time in your practice.

2: Make Meditation Habitual

Try to create positive associations with meditation. Let your meditation space have a close link to the relaxation response you desire. The space should be as calming as possible, but

Meditation For Beginners

not necessarily fancy. Try to practice in the same place and at the same time each day.

3: Try Group Meditation

Gather a few trusted friends and try to be accountable to each other. Your friends will help you schedule for meditation time and remain loyal during the sessions. This is because you are inclined to stick to meditation if you are in a group. After all, you would not want to be the jerk that makes a lot of noise scooting around or the one who gives up in the middle of the session. Remember, human beings portray their best behavior when in the midst of their peers. Eventually, this behavior will evolve to be normal during meditation, which will then help you enjoy meditation sessions even when you are alone.

4: Understand What Meditation Is All About

You may be tempted to believe that meditation is all about dictating where you should focus without getting distracted. However, meditation's main goal is to help you become aware of when your mind drifts. Thus, you need to become aware of what you are thinking so that you can restructure your thoughts. Meditation helps you gain the ability to identify your thoughts. Moreover, as a beginner your primary goal should be gaining the ability to redirect your attention to your point of focus without necessarily faulting or criticizing yourself.

5: Practice Breath Control

Meditation For Beginners

By learning how to control your breath, you will be able to control how your brain responds to stressful situations. You can develop your breath control as follows:

1. Start by breathing in for 8 seconds, hold it for 4 seconds, breathe out for 8 seconds, and then hold for 4 seconds. You can practice this for 5 minutes each morning and evening and gradually increase the practice time from there. Also, do these calming repetitions whenever you feel anxious.

2. Progress to breathing in for 12 seconds, holding for 6 seconds, and then breathing out for 12 seconds before holding for 6 seconds; this can form the basis of your meditation practice. Continue practicing breath control: do it when driving, while queuing for any service, or even while sitting at your office desk. Also, dedicate a few minutes of each day to focusing on breathing and feeling the expansion and contraction of your lungs. This exercise has a cumulative effect, with each session building on the previous one as it reconfigures your body systems accordingly.

Always keep in mind that meditation plays a major role in reducing the release of stress related hormones and increasing your brain's parasympathetic activity. Keep practicing how to calm your mind and know how to direct your attention to a single point of focus. To stay in the present, learn how to feel the various body sensations as they rise.

6: Don't Expect Too Much Too Soon

One of the biggest mistakes most novices make while meditating is the amount of expectations they associate with the practice. Upon hearing great things about meditation, it is only likely that you expect the practice to do wonders for you like magic. Two minutes into the practice and you look forward to becoming sage and intuitive. Sadly, this is far from reality.

Meditation does help you relax and unlock spiritual awakening, but it takes time. Just like you cannot lose 20 pounds within days, you cannot become spiritually awakened and mindful within minutes too. The mindful state of mind can be unlocked and tapped into, but that will take time. You need to be patient with yourself and consistent with the practice to achieve that result. Trust the process and be persistent with it to gradually move towards this point. You need to engage in the practice daily for 2 to 5 minutes in the start only and gradually increase the duration of the practice to hone on it and yield better results. If you just work on that, you will achieve your desired results soon enough.

7: Don't Quit Too Soon

A common mistake that most meditation newbies make when practicing is to quit too soon. This does not mean that you should not engage in a short, 2 to 5 minute practice. It means that you must not quit the practice the moment you get fidgety, distracted or bored because if you keep quitting it every instant you feel distracted and frustrated, you will not be able to push yourself to reach the deep, meditative state. Even if you meditate for a 2 minute practice, you will feel distracted in it several times because you haven't trained yourself to focus on anything yet. You need to bring back your focus to the practice every time it is shattered. If you keep trying to realign your focus and be mindful of the practice even if it is for 2 seconds, you will slowly and gradually be able to unlock the state of mindfulness. As long as you keep bringing your attention to the practice, you are being mindful of it and this determination is what you need to be better at meditation.

8: Make it Fun

Meditation does not have to be boring or annoying. You cannot nurture its habit if you find the practice tedious and have to force yourself to sit down for it even if it is for 2 minutes. You need to make it fun and engaging for yourself to become enthusiastic about it and that can be done through different ways.

Ask a friend to do meditate with you a couple of times in the week and both of you can share your experiences with one another in the end. You can also light up sweet smelling incense in your meditative spot to make the experience pleasant for yourself. You can even find interesting soundtracks to listen to while meditating; or you can pick a fun object such as your baby or any of your childhood toys to observe without holding any bias for the chosen object and learn new things about it. The more you start to enjoy the experience, the more likelier you will stick to it in the long run.

9: Immerse Yourself in the Experience

You become more aware of the moment and mindful of your surroundings when you completely immerse yourself in the experience, and this happens effectively when you completely engage your 5 senses in the experience. If you are simply observing your breath, you need to completely engage all your 5 senses in it by focusing on the feeling of your breath; any odor you can smell or imagine what a sensation may smell like; any sound you hear when your breath moves in and out of your body; any taste you can feel; and imagining how your breath maybe moving inside your body to engage your sense of sight. When each of your 5 senses becomes engaged in the act, you feel alive from within and focus better on the practice.

10: Have a Pre-Meditation Routine

Having a pre-meditation routine before starting off with the actual meditation practice is crucial to strengthen your state of mindfulness and benefit better from the practice. Just like you need to do some warm up exercises prior to kick-starting your actual workout, you need to have a pre-meditation routine to warm yourself up for the main meditative practice and carry it out with ease. So if you want to do mindfulness meditation for 10 minutes, take deep breaths for 2 minutes and focus on your breath. You can do anything relaxing and grounding in your pre-meditation routine to feel calmer and more focused on the present.

11: Ask Yourself Powerful and Thought Provoking Questions

A common misconception about meditation is to completely silence your mind and eliminate every type of thought from it. While meditation does calm your racing mind and encourages you to focus on one thing at a time, it does not in any way focus on emptying your mind of thoughts. When you meditate and are able to carry out the practice for 10 minutes straight, ask yourself powerful, strong and thought provoking questions aimed at better understanding yourself and your life. Try to uncover the reality of things by questioning the authenticity of things and trying to dig deeper into more than what meets the eye. Remember to be unbiased throughout that time and accept everything openly.

Consistency is the key to yield compound effects; therefore, ensure that you work on these tips and tricks every time you meditate. To further enhance the effectiveness of the practice, incorporate some mudras in your meditative practice.

Chapter 7: Mudras to Strengthen the Effectiveness of Meditation

Mudras are simple hand positions that reinforce certain healing states of your mind to bring about the desired outcome. For years it was believed and now this belief is backed by science that there exist nerves in our fingers and hands that connect to different centers in our brain. These connections when triggered bring about different results in our bodies and minds helping us achieve desired outcomes. This means you can use simple hand positions to be happy, feel peaceful and get rid of stress. Mudras can be practiced alone or while meditating to enhance the effectiveness of both, meditation and the mudra.

According to Sah D'Simone, a meditation teacher and expert, mudras are a great way to draw mindfulness inward and establish a connection between your heart and soul. They also fill you with compassion, positivity, goodness, awareness and pure joy. Each of your five fingers symbolizes a particular element. Your thumb stands for space, index finger represents air, middle finger signifies fire, the ring finger stands for water; and your pinky indicates earth. When you connect different fingers together, you combine different elements that stabilize different irregularities in your body and help you feel peaceful, happy and achieve whatever outcome you desire. Here are 9 amazing mudras that can do wonders for you.

Varada Mudra

This mudra evokes compassion, generosity and creativity. If you wish to hone on your empathy and become a compassionate, giving and loving individual, practice this mudra while chanting a kindness based mantra.

To practice it, rest your left hand on the left knee with your palm facing upwards. Extend your fingers upwards and place your right hand on your thigh, knee or lap. Maintain this for 2 to 5 minutes to achieve the desired outcome. The image below shows a statue of Buddha practicing the varada mudra.

Samadhi Mudra

This mudra is excellent in initiating a deep state of concentration. Also referred to as 'dhyana mudra', it supports focus and clarity. If you often find yourself wandering off in thought while meditating or have trouble concentrating on a task, practice Samadhi mudra daily while meditating and otherwise for 5 minutes.

To practice it, rest both your hands on the lap ensuring that your palms face upwards. Your right hand must be placed on the top of your left one and the tips of both your thumbs must lightly touch one another.

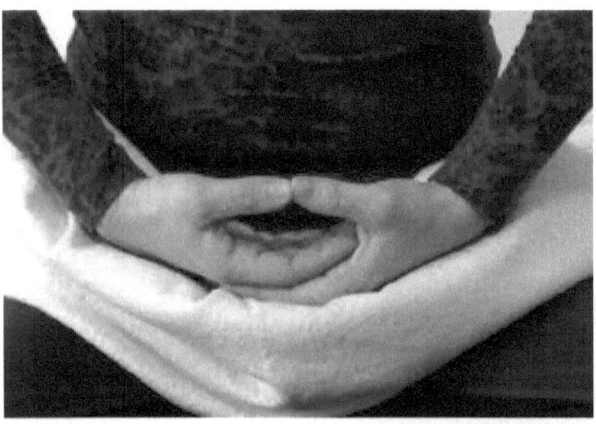

Karana Mudra

This mudra works well in warding off negativity, toxicity and helping you attain inner peace. To practice it, touch your middle finger of the right hand with your thumb and then extend your pinky and index fingers. Bring the right hand in front of your heart and keep the palms facing out. Your left hand can rest on your lap. Maintain this for 2 minutes at least while meditating to promote a positive state of mind and focus on the happy things in life.

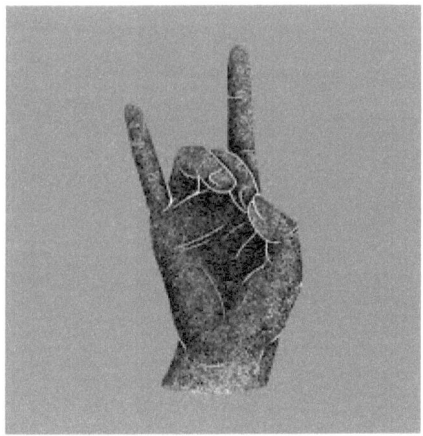

Jnana Mudra

This is a fantastic mudra to enhance your knowledge and wisdom of things. If you wish to be better at memorizing things, want to enhance your cognition and unlock your ability to better analyze things, this is the mudra to practice regularly.

To practice it, curl the index fingers towards the end of your thumbs and make a circle. Your remaining fingers need to extend straight and the palms should rest on the knees facing upwards or downwards. Maintain this for 5 minutes daily particularly when meditating on powerful thoughts to promote increased clarity and wisdom.

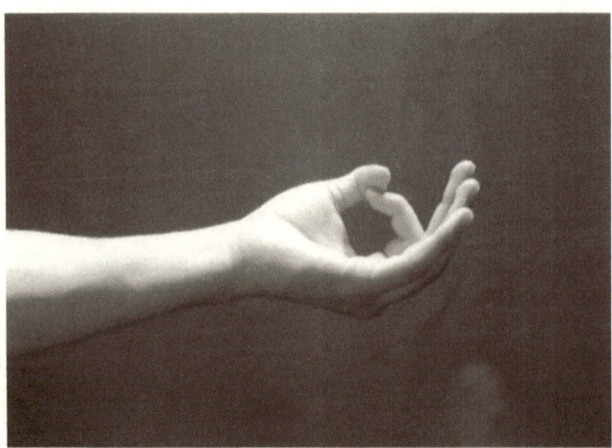

Varuna Mudra

This mudra balances the water element in your body. It is great for relieving indigestion and constipation and helps you stay fit and healthy. Join the tips of the thumbs with the tips of your pinky fingers while extending the rest of your fingers outward. Place the hands with palms facing upwards on the knees.

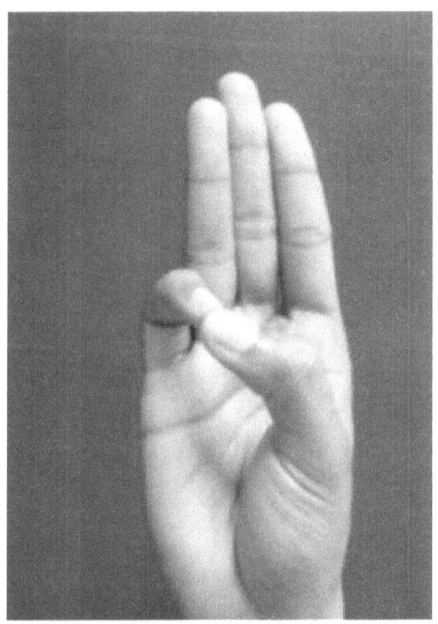

Gyan Mudra

This is one of the most commonly practiced mudras of all times and works really well in enhancing your cognition, intuition and ability to think deeply. It works exceptionally well in combination with mindfulness meditation and transcendental meditation. To exercise it, touch your index finger with your thumb and extend the other three fingers. Practice it for 5 minutes or for as long as you meditate to unlock the peace and wisdom you have been missing out on in your life.

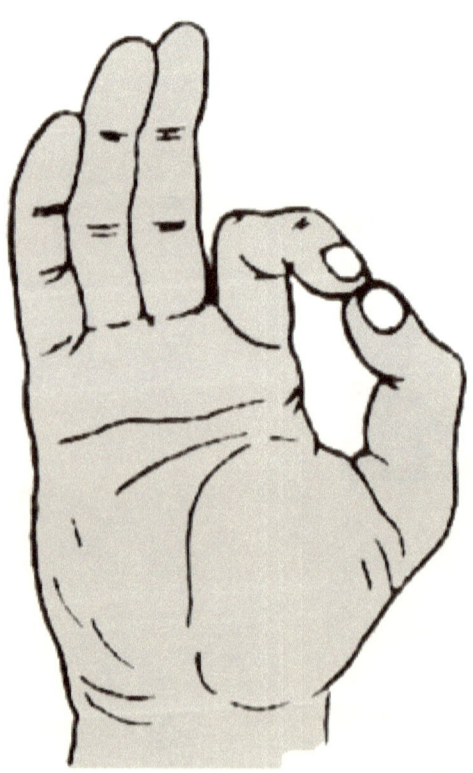

Prana Mudra

Prana refers to the vital life force that we need to stay alive. It is the energy that circulates inside us that helps us survive and perform optimally. The prana mudra opens up the prana channels throughout the body and allows you to get rid of all the toxins and negative energy that has been holding you back.

The stress, depression, anxiety, emotional issues and several other problems we experience in life including relationship, professional and financial problems are due to the blockage of prana in our body and mind. It is this blockage that keeps us from achieving clarity in life that affects our decision making abilities.

In addition, when there is irregular energy circulation in your body, you will grow weaker and sicker with time. To get rid of all these problems, practice the prana mudra for at least 5 minutes twice daily.

To practice it, touch your thumb's tip with the tips of your pinky and ring fingers, and extend the other two fingers. You can do it while meditating to combine its power with that of meditation, or you can even do it separately.

Meditation For Beginners

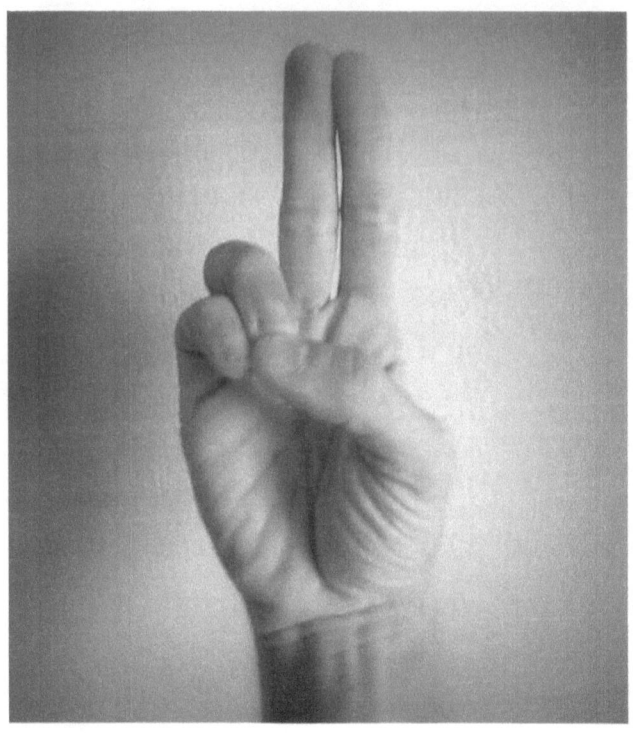

Apana Mudra

The apana mudra is another great mudra to practice to achieve complete emotional, psychological and physical wellbeing. It like the prana mudra improves the circulation of energy in your body and removes all sorts of irregularities. It improves the digestion process and aids in the smooth elimination of toxic elements from your body. To practice it, touch your thumb's tip with your ring and middle fingers and extend the remaining two fingers. Practice it for 2 to 5 minutes several times throughout the day especially while meditating.

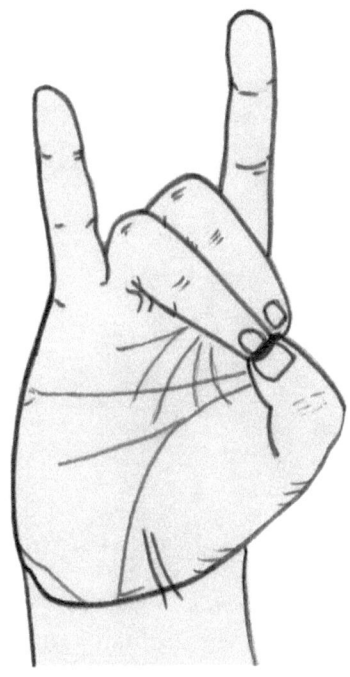

Shuni Mudra

Shuni mudra works wonders in helping you attain the clarity missing out from your life. It opens up your mind to possibilities, knowledge, wisdom and intuition in unimaginable ways and you start to understand things better. This is a fantastic mudra to practice when meditating on your life's vision and sense of direction. Practice it by joining the tip of your thumb with that of your middle finger and maintain it for 5 minutes.

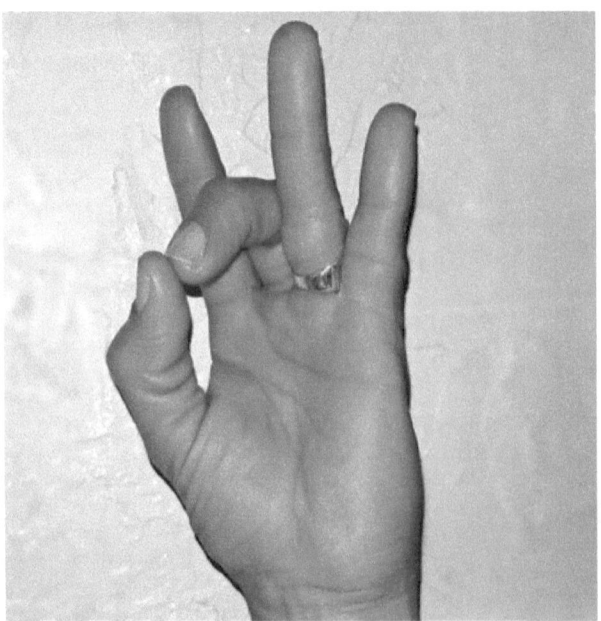

You can start off by incorporating one or two of these mudras into your daily meditation practice depending on the outcomes you are trying to achieve. If you want clarity in life, try shuni or gyan mudra first, but if your emotional and physical wellbeing is your topmost priority right now, opt for prana or apana mudra. Slowly, try to bring in all the mudras discussed above in different meditative practices to unlock complete clarity in all areas of life and achieve complete wellbeing.

Conclusion

We have come to the end of the book. Thank you for reading and congratulations for reading until the end.

The power of meditation lies in how you discipline your mind. You can meditate from anywhere as long as your mind is devoid of distractions. Let the ritualistic side of meditation not hinder you from reaping it immense benefits. Be consistent and maintain a good attitude.

If you found the book valuable, can you recommend it to others? One way to do that is to post a review on Amazon.

Click here to leave a review for this book on Amazon!

Thank you and good luck!

Do You Like My Book & Approach To Publishing?

If you like my writing and style and would love the ease of learning literally everything you can get your hands on from Fantonpublishers.com, I'd really need you to do me either of the following favors.

1: First, I'd Love It If You Leave a Review of This Book on Amazon.

2: Check Out My Emotional Mastery Books

Emotional Intelligence: The Mindfulness Guide To Mastering Your Emotions, Getting Ahead And Improving Your Life

Stress: The Psychology of Managing Pressure: Practical Strategies to turn Pressure into Positive Energy (5 Key Stress Techniques for Stress, Anxiety, and Depression Relief)

Failure Is Not The END: It Is An Emotional Gym: Complete Workout Plan On How To Build Your Emotional Muscle And Burning Down Anxiety To Become Emotionally Stronger, More Confident and Less Reactive

Subconscious Mind: Tame, Reprogram & Control Your Subconscious Mind To Transform Your Life

Body Language: Master Body Language: A Practical Guide to Understanding Nonverbal Communication and Improving Your Relationships

Shame and Guilt: Overcoming Shame and Guilt: Step By Step Guide On How to Overcome Shame and Guilt for Good

Anger Management: A Simple Guide on How to Deal with Anger

Get updates when we publish any book that will help you master your emotions: http://bit.ly/2fantonpubpersonaldevl

To get a list of all my other books, visit my author page or let me send you the list by requesting them below: http://bit.ly/2fantonpubnewbooks

3: Grab Some Freebies On Your Way Out; Giving Is Receiving, Right?

I gave you a complimentary book at the start of the book. If you are still interested, grab it here.

5 Pillar Life Transformation Checklist: http://bit.ly/2fantonfreebie

www.ingramcontent.com/pod-product-compliance
Lightning Source LLC
Chambersburg PA
CBHW030159100526
44592CB00009B/359